The Ant Chant

The Magical Power of Determination

Written by
Michal Y. Noah, Ph.D.

Illustrated by
Favreau

Text and Illustrations Copyright © 2016 by Michal Y. Noah

All rights reserved. No part of this publication may be reproduced, distributed, or transmitted in any form or by any means, including photocopying, recording, or other electronic or mechanical methods, without the prior written permission of the publisher, except in the case of brief quotations embodied in critical reviews and cer‹tain other noncommercial uses permitted by copyright law. For permission requests, write to the publisher, addressed "Attention: Permissions Coordinator," at the address below.

A Magical World in You, Inc.
Huntingdon Valley, PA 19006
www.michalynoah.com

Hardcover ISBN 978-0-9967757-0-0
Paperback ISBN 978-0-9967757-2-4

Library of Congress Control Number: 2016915431

This is a work of fiction. Names, characters, businesses, places, events and incidents are either the products of the author's imagination or used in a fictitious manner. Any resemblance to actual persons, living or dead, or actual events is purely coincidental.

Ordering Information:

Quantity sales. Special discounts are available on quantity purchases by corporations, associations, and others. For details, contact the publisher at the address above.

Printed in the United States of America.

AUTHOR'S NOTE

I truly believe that the seed for greatness lies within all of us, that we have the magic to create the life that we desire and are born to live. I do know that in order to achieve this, there is an important ingredient needed – the right mindset with a positive attitude and a strong determination to reach one's goal.

Obstacles and challenges are part of life. It is important to teach children from a young age how to cope when faced with setbacks. The key is to carry on and overcome the challenges with joyful determination, using the power of self-talk by chanting simple words of self-encouragement.

I wrote this fifth book, *The Ant Chant*, especially to illustrate this simple life lesson. There is much we can learn by observing the little ant who never gives up, despite insurmountable roadblocks and impediments on her journey. A firm believer in staying focused, the little ant relies on determination, persistence and team-work to achieve her object.

Moreover, as states Napoleon Hill, "You are the master of your destiny. You can influence, direct, and control your own environment. You can make your life what you want it to be."

Michal Noah

On a beautiful morning,
With not a speck of gray,
One little ant decides
"Today I won't go and play."

"There's no time to lose,
First it's work, and then it's play,
Lots and lots for me to do,
On this lovely, sunny day."

"I'll search for food,
Then I'll cart it away.
I just want to have fun,
Once I'm done, I'll play."

"Oh, I plan to enjoy
And have lots of fun,
As I work outside,
In the warmth of the sun."

Determined she goes,
Walking tall and strong,
All eager and excited,
Singing a cheerful song.

"I've got a special magic,
When I work, I chant,
I can do anything,
I'm a joyful little ant."

"Though I'm a wee little ant,
I am strong and wise.
I stay focused, you see,
On my goal, I keep my eyes."

She continues her march,
A smile on her face,
"It may not be so easy,
But every challenge I embrace."

Suddenly she stops,
"Look what I just found!"
She shouts in excitement,
"There's food on the ground!"

There are nuts and berries
Some grains, fruits and seeds.
Our Ant feels happy,
Yes, it's just what she needs.

"OK, I'm going to try to pick it up!
One – Two – Three.
I'll first take a deep breath,
Yes, there's strength in me!"

The tiny grain of food
Is twice the little ant's size,
Yet she looks happy,
"Feels like I won a prize!"

"I'm a tiny little ant,
I'm wise and strong,
I'm happy to be working,
All – day – long."

Our busy little ant,
Continues her song,
Singing so joyfully,
"I'm getting strong!"

She's cheerful and happy,
On her face there's a smile,
The joyful ant says,
"I'll put all this in a pile."

It's a lot for her to carry
She calls out, "Come, quick!"
Her friends they come running,
And gladly take their pick.

"We'll quickly take this home
And with a smile on our face,
We'll store it for a rainy day,
In our secret hiding place."

"Back to work I go now,
Much still to do today,
It may not be so easy,
But I'll do my best, anyway."

"I am just a little ant,
I am wise, I am strong.
Happily I keep working,
While singing my song."

"Oh, I never ever quit,
This is my chant, my song!
I am so determined,
That I just can't go wrong."

"Nothing will stop me,
I am strong, I am wise,
Never ever give up,
Is what I always advise."

"If there's a challenge,
I'll figure out a way.
I won't allow anything
To ruin my day."

"Just a few hours of work,
A morning well spent,
Time has flown so fast,
The day just came and went."

"My work is finally complete,
I feel truly satisfied,
So much I have accomplished,
In my dedication, I take pride."

"It's time for me to rest a bit,
After all that I have done today,
I smile as I now take a break,
And off I go to play."

OTHER BOOKS BY MICHAL NOAH

A-Z: The Universe in Me

The Magic Tree

I'll See You in My Dreams

Sparkles

www.ingramcontent.com/pod-product-compliance
Lightning Source LLC
Chambersburg PA
CBHW061932290426
44113CB00024B/2883